Science
made easy

Key Stage 2
Ages 8–9

Authors Linda Ellis, David Evans,
Mike Evans and Hugh Westrup
Consultants Sean McArdle and Kara Pranikoff

Certificate

Congratulations to ....
<small>(write your name here)</small>
for successfully finishing this book.

☆ *You're a star!* ☆

Is it an animal or a plant?

Science facts

Plants and animals are living things. Animals usually move from place to place to find food. Animals are sensitive to their surroundings and usually respond quickly to changes. Plants are green and usually rooted to the ground. They do not need to move to feed because they make their own food. Plants respond to light by growing towards its source.

Science quiz

These living things look very much alike. Write the letter **P** in the boxes beside the ones you think are plants. Write the letter **A** in the boxes beside the ones you think are animals.

A sea anemone captures food with its tentacles. It moves slowly.

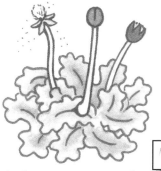

A liverwort makes its own food and does not move.

A feather star uses its arms to move from place to place to find food.

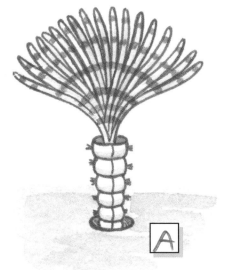

A peacock worm moves up and down in its tube and catches food with its tentacles.

Moss is green and makes its own food.

Science activity

(!) Germinate some mung beans. When the bean seedlings develop their first leaves, place them in a shoebox. Put the lid on the box. Ask an adult to cut a slit on one side, so that light can get in. What do you think the seedlings will look like after a few days?

What kind of animal is it?

Science facts

It is easy to see how one animal is different from another. It is more difficult to say how animals are alike. We can put animals into groups according to the features they have in common. For example, animals that can keep their body warm, lay eggs, do not have teeth, have feathers on their body and scales on their legs belong to the group of animals we call birds.

Science quiz

What features do the animals in each group have in common?
What is the name of each group of animals?

Common features of group A animals:

......they have warm blood......

......they all have some......

......gio hair they give......

......birth to live young......

These animals are ....mammals....

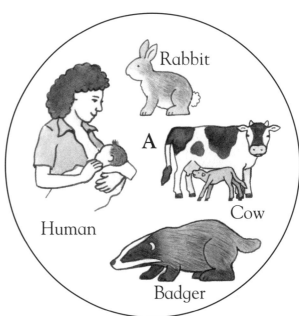

Rabbit

A

Cow

Human

Badger

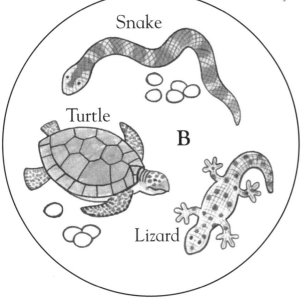

Snake

Turtle

B

Lizard

Common features of group B animals:

......they have cold bloo they......

......say eggs they have scales......

....

....

These animals are ....reptiles........

Science activity

Collect together as many different kinds of coin as you can. Sort them into groups. What features do the coins in each group have in common?

What kind of plant is it?

Science facts

It is easy to see how one plant is different from another. It is more difficult to say how plants are alike. We can put plants into groups according to the features they have in common. For example, the plants we call mosses produce spores, have green bodies that often look like leaves and have thin parts to hold the plants in the soil.

Science quiz

What features do the plants in each group have in common? What is the name of each group of plants?

Cypress

Fir

A

Pine

Common features of group A plants:

....

....

....

....

These plants are .....*pion tres*

Common features of group B plants:

ther are couldful

bees Take grom then

....

....

These plants are .....*flover*

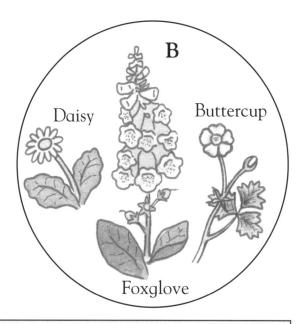

B

Daisy

Buttercup

Foxglove

Science activity

Compare two different types of flower. Write down as many ways as you can in which they are different and as many ways as you can in which they are the same.

Are you an animal detective?

Science facts

An animal key helps you identify different animals. If you don't know an animal's name, a key will give you all the clues you need. Solve the clues one by one and you will discover the name of the animal, just like a detective solving a mystery.

Science quiz

Follow this Yes/No animal key to find the names of the insects in the pictures.

Clue 1   Does the insect have very large eyes? If yes, go to clue 2.
Does the insect have small eyes? If yes, go to clue 3.

Clue 2   Are the insect's eyes touching? If yes, it is a dragonfly.
If the insect's eyes are not touching, it is a damselfly.

Clue 3   Does the head have a long pointed beak? If yes, it is a scorpion fly.
If the head does not have a pointed beak, go to clue 4.

Clue 4   Does the insect have three tails? If yes, it is a mayfly.
Does the insect have only one tail? If yes, it is a lacewing.

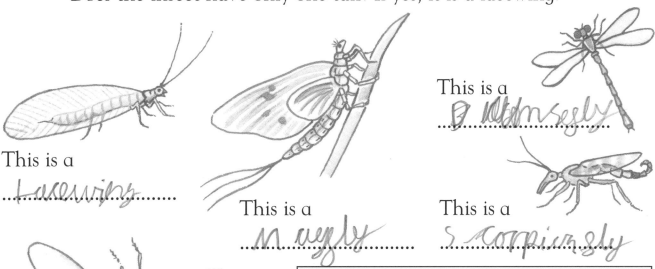

This is a
Lacewing

This is a
mayfly

This is a
D. damselfly

This is a
S. corpionfly

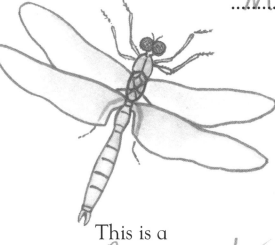

This is a
D. dragonfly

Science activity

Where do the insects in the pictures live? What do they eat? How long does a mayfly live? Use books and the Internet to help you find the answers.

5

Are you a plant detective?

Science facts

By using a plant key, you can become a plant detective and discover the names of different plants. A plant key gives you all the clues you need to identify a plant. The key shown below is called a branching key. If you follow the branch that describes what you see, it will lead you to the plant's name.

Science quiz

Use this branching Yes/No key to find the names of these fruits.

A...*Banana*... B...*Apple*... C...*pear*... D...*Grapefruit*... E...*grape*... F...*orange*...

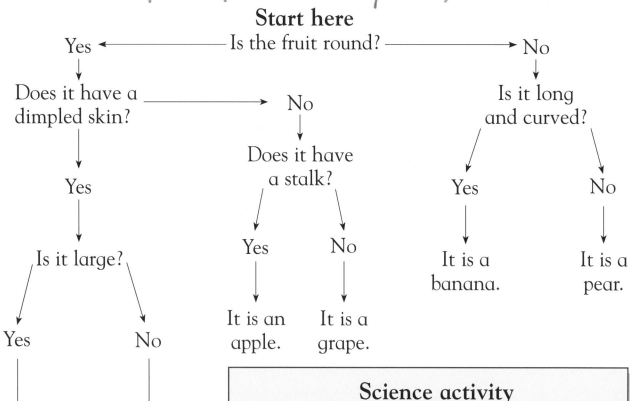

Start here

Yes ← Is the fruit round? → No

Does it have a dimpled skin? ——→ No

Is it long and curved?

Yes

Does it have a stalk?

Is it large?

Yes   No

It is an apple.   It is a grape.

Yes   No

Yes   No

It is a banana.   It is a pear.

Yes   No

It is a grapefruit.   It is an orange.

Science activity

How many differences can you think of between a carrot and a potato? Make a list of them. Do the same for an onion and a garlic bulb.

What happens when things die?

Science facts

Animals such as earthworms feed on dead plants. Other animals, such as maggots, feed on dead animals. There are also tiny living things called micro-organisms that feed on dead animals and plants. Bacteria and many types of fungus are micro-organisms. They cause dead things to decay.

Science quiz

Here are some animals found in woodlands, where there are decaying leaves. Can you use this Yes/No key to find their names?

Clue 1 Does the animal have six legs? If yes, it is a springtail.
        Does the animal have more than six legs? If yes, go to clue 2.

Clue 2 Does it have eight legs? If yes, it is a harvestman.
        Does it have more than eight legs? If yes, go to clue 3.

Clue 3 Does it have a broad, flat body? If yes, it is a woodlouse.
        Does it have a long, thin body? If yes, go to clue 4.

Clue 4 Does each section of the body have two legs? If yes, it is a centipede.
        Does each section of the body have four legs? If yes, it is a millipede.

This is a ....

This is a ...Harvestman...

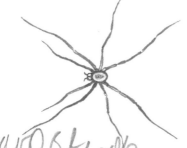

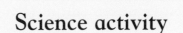

This is a ...springtail...

This is a ....

This is a ....

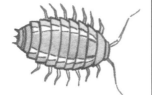

Science activity

(!) Bury an apple core in the ground. What do you think will happen to the apple core if you leave it buried, and why? Dig up the core after three weeks to see whether your prediction is correct.

What animal lives where?

Science facts

Animals come in many different shapes and sizes. Most animals live in one type of habitat because they are suited to it. They are adapted to suit the environment in which they live. For example, many frogs, newts and toads have webbed feet to help them swim in their watery habitat. Squirrels have sharp claws to grip and long tails to help them balance as they scramble up and down trees.

Science quiz

Look at these pictures. Explain how each animal is adapted to its habitat.

A desert fox lives in hot, dry places.

....
....

A mole burrows in dark underground tunnels.

....
....

An arctic fox lives in cold places.

....
....

A dormouse is active at night. It climbs shrubs and trees.

....
....

Science activity

Can you find some animals in your garden or local park? Make a list of the animals and the places where you found them. Write some notes about the ways in which each animal is suited to where it lives.

What plant lives where?

Science facts

Plants are suited, or adapted, to the different habitats in which they grow. Those growing on land usually have stiff stems to hold them upright, while water plants tend to have weaker stems because the water supports them. Plants in hot, dry places often have short or few leaves so that they do not lose too much water. Some also store water in thick stems. Plants growing in shaded areas often have large leaves to trap as much sunlight as possible.

Science quiz

Look at the drawings below. Explain how each plant is suited to its habitat.

A cactus growing in a hot, dry area.

....

....

Pond weed growing just under the surface of water.

....

A daisy growing in mowed or grazed grass.

....

....

Look at these two dandelion plants. Which one do you think grew underneath a tree? Why?

....

....

Science activity

(!) Explore some woodland or shaded parts of a garden with an adult. Can you find any difference between plants such as dandelions and nettles growing under bushes or trees and those growing in open areas?

How do we affect living things?

Science facts

The activities of humans can affect the lives of animals and plants. Pollution from factories and cars can poison the air and water that animals and plants need to survive. The places where they feed and reproduce are often used to build houses and shops. Humans need places to live and work, but there must be a balance between human needs and the needs of animals and plants.

Science quiz

Draw a circle around each thing in this picture that could cause harm to animals and plants.

Science activity

Put a clean piece of white paper outside. It should be in the open air but in a place that is sheltered from the rain. Put a mug on top of the paper. What do you think the paper will look like after a week? What will you find when you lift up the mug?

What is the digestive system?

Science facts
The digestive system turns food into nutrients that our bodies need to survive.

Science quiz
Use the words in the box to complete the sentences.

Oesophagus	Large intestine	Mouth	Small intestine	Stomach

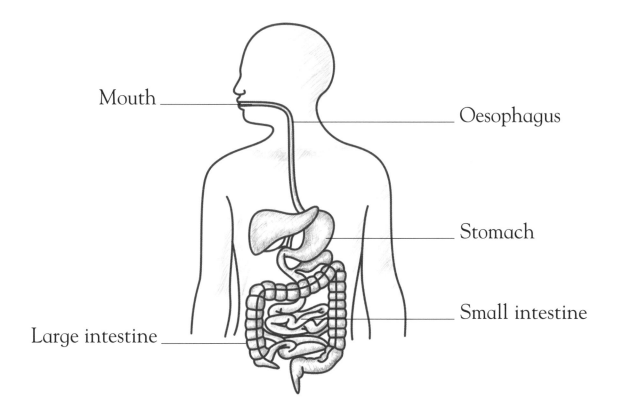

Mouth

Oesophagus

Stomach

Small intestine

Large intestine

1 The digestion process begins in the .... , where food is chewed and mixed with saliva.

2 The .... connects the mouth to the stomach.

3 The .... contains an acid fluid that breaks down food.

4 The .... is a long tube where nutrients from digested food pass into the bloodstream.

5 The .... absorbs water from food and turns the parts of food that you can't digest into waste.

What do our teeth do?

Science facts

Humans have four different types of tooth. Young children have about 20 teeth, called milk teeth. They have eight teeth called incisors at the front of the mouth (four above and four below). These are used for cutting food. The next four sharp, pointed teeth are the canines, which are used for tearing food. Next to these are the premolars, used for grinding and chewing. Between the ages of five and ten years, these milk teeth are replaced by adult ones, which include another twelve teeth called molars. These are also used for chewing.

Science quiz

Animals that eat meat have sharp, pointed teeth called canines and scissor-like teeth called premolars and molars to cut and tear meat. Animals that eat plants have large, flat molars for grinding and chewing. Humans eat both meat and plants. What sort of teeth do humans have? Label each type of tooth shown in the diagram below.

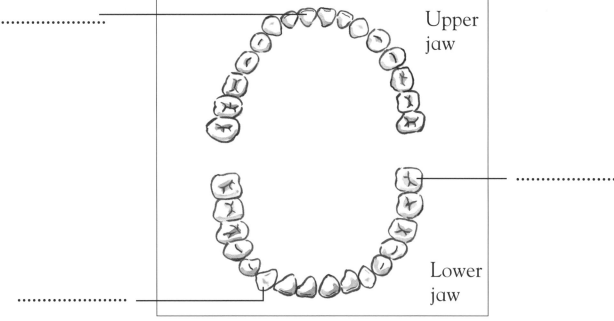

....

Upper jaw

....

Lower jaw

....

A set of adult human teeth

Science activity

Use a mirror to look inside your own mouth. Then, in the diagram above, colour in all the teeth that you have. You may not have all the teeth in the diagram as it shows an adult's teeth. Check with your friends and some adults to see if they have the same number of teeth as you.

What causes tooth decay?

Science facts

When we chew food, some of it becomes stuck between our teeth. Tiny living things in our mouths, called bacteria, attack this food and feed on it themselves. As the bacteria feed, they produce acid, which can decay our teeth. By cleaning our teeth after meals, the bits of food are brushed away so the bacteria cannot feed and produce acid.

Science quiz

A class of children were expecting to see the school dentist. Their teacher asked them to do a survey of how often they cleaned their teeth. The block graph below shows the results of their survey.

How often we clean our teeth

Never						
Not very often	Sean	Sam				
Sometimes	James	Amy				
Most days	Oliver	Aziz	Emily	Maria		
Twice each day	Mina	John	Ling	Emma	Earl	Rachel

Which children are most likely to need treatment from the dentist?

....

Science activity

Which is the best way of cleaning your teeth: eating an apple, rinsing with water or brushing then rinsing? Ask an adult to help you use disclosing tablets to test the three ways of cleaning. (Disclosing tablets reveal bacteria in the mouth.)

Are animal teeth the same as ours?

Science facts
You have different teeth for doing different jobs. The sharp front teeth, called incisors, bite and cut up food. The flat back teeth, called molars, grind up food before it is swallowed. You also have pointed teeth near the front of your mouth that grip, pierce and tear food. These are called canines. Animals such as tigers and lions have large canines to catch and kill their prey.

Science quiz
An animal's skull clearly shows its teeth. Look at the teeth on the rabbit skull and the cat skull below.

Rabbit skull

Cat skull

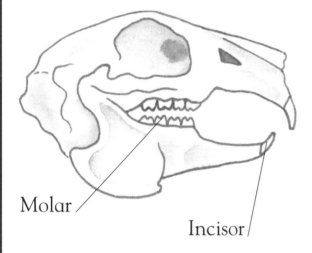

Molar

Incisor

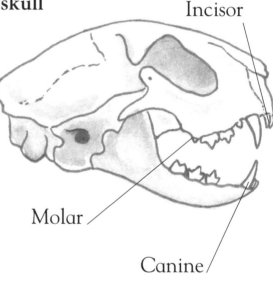

Incisor

Molar

Canine

Why does the rabbit have large incisors?

....

Why doesn't the rabbit have canines?

....

How can you tell that the cat catches and eats other animals?

....

Why does the cat have such small incisors?

....

....

Science activity

Using a small mirror, count how many teeth you have. How many of each type are there? Do you have teeth like a meat-eating carnivore or a plant-eating herbivore?

Is it a food chain?

Science facts

Plants and seaweeds can make their own food. They are called producers. Herbivores eat plants to obtain proteins, carbohydrates and fats. They use these nutrients to grow and for energy. Carnivores eat herbivores and use the meat in the same way. Carnivores are called predators and the animals they eat are called prey. There is a chain from plants, to herbivores that eat plants, to carnivores that eat herbivores. This is called a food chain.

Science quiz

Look at the pictures and find the animals or plants that complete these food chains. Write their names in the spaces on the chart.

Plant makes food	Herbivore eats plant	Carnivore eats herbivore
Pansy	....	Thrush
Seaweed	Periwinkle	....
....	Caterpillar	Robin
Grass	....	....

Seagull

Slug

Oak leaf

Human

Cow

Science activity

Many birds are herbivores, but some are carnivores. Draw and label a food chain that includes a bird as a herbivore. Draw another chain showing a bird as a carnivore.

What is a food chain?

Science facts

A food chain is the feeding relationship between different plants and animals in a particular environment, or habitat. A plant is nearly always at the start of a food chain because it produces food. It is called a producer. Consumers are animals that eat producers or other consumers. The animal in a food chain that eats the producer is called the first consumer. The animal that eats the first consumer is called the second consumer, and so on. The direction of arrows between the organisms in a food chain shows what is eaten by what.

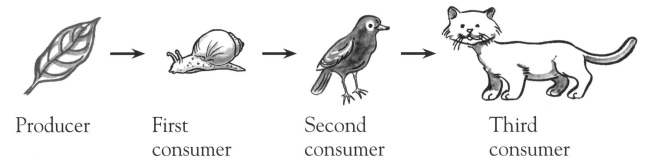

Producer   First   Second   Third
               consumer   consumer   consumer

Science quiz

Look at the two food chains below. Identify the producer, first consumer and second consumer in each food chain. Write your answers in the table.

A   Plant plankton → Water flea → Stickleback → Dragonfly larva → Pike

B   Water plant → Water snails → Water-beetle larva → Frog → Heron

Food chain	Producer	First consumer	Second consumer
A	....	....	....
B	....	....	....

Science activity

Write these words on some cards: **Plant material**, **Carp** (a fish that feeds on plant material), **Heron** (a bird that feeds on fish) and **Pike** (a fish that feeds on other fish). Now make a food chain by placing the cards in order and by putting some arrow cards in the correct direction between them.

Is it solid?

Science facts

Materials are either solids, liquids or gases. You can recognise solid materials by their properties. Solids do not change shape by themselves and you cannot push your finger through them easily. Solids do not make things wet.

Science quiz

Look at the materials below. Put a tick (✔) beside each one that you think is a solid.
Hint: for materials such as sand and salt, think about the individual grains.

Modelling clay ☐

Aluminium
kitchen foil ☐

Wood ☐

Sand ☐

Salt ☐

Marbles ☐

Science activity

! Whisk the white of an egg until it becomes stiff. What happens if you leave it for a while? When you boil an egg, the egg white becomes solid. What happens if you leave the egg white for a while?

How runny is it?

Science facts

Liquids are materials that make things wet. All liquids flow. This means that they are runny and you can pour them. If you spill liquids, they spread out. A liquid will fill a container, such as a bottle. If you leave a liquid to stand, its surface will become level. You can easily push your finger through a liquid.

Science quiz

A class of children did an experiment to find out which of the five liquids below was the runniest. The same amount of each liquid was poured from a jug into a glass. The time it took to fill each glass was written down.

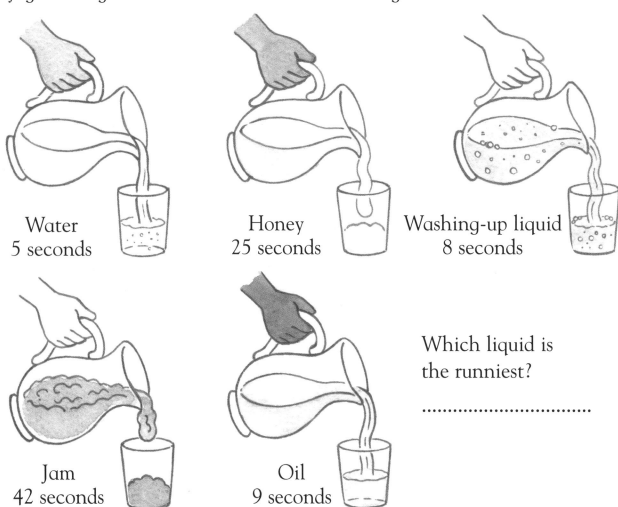

Water
5 seconds

Honey
25 seconds

Washing-up liquid
8 seconds

Jam
42 seconds

Oil
9 seconds

Which liquid is
the runniest?

....

Science activity

If you drop a marble into a glass of honey and another into a glass of treacle at the same time, which one will reach the bottom first? Which liquid is runnier?

Is it gassy?

Science facts

Gases are usually colourless and invisible. They spread out to fill containers, such as balloons. Gases form bubbles when they mix with liquids. The air you breathe contains gases called oxygen, carbon dioxide and nitrogen. You know they are there because you can blow bubbles in water with a straw. You cannot see them, but you can feel them blowing against your face in windy weather.

Science quiz

A scientist filled three balloons with different gases. He tied the ends so that the gases could not escape. He held them up and released them all at once. The balloon filled with carbon dioxide fell to the ground quickly. The one filled with helium floated upwards. The one filled with air fell slowly to the ground.

Helium

Air

Use the words **heavier** and **lighter** to fill in the gaps and complete each of the sentences.

Carbon dioxide is .... than air.

Helium is .... than air.

Helium is .... than carbon dioxide.

Carbon dioxide

Science activity

Mix washing-up liquid with water and sugar. Bend a pipe cleaner into a ring shape. Dip it in the mixture and use it to blow bubbles. What happens if you make the ring bigger? What now happens if you change the ring into a square?

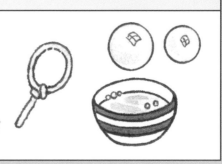

What kind of material is it?

Science facts

Materials can exist as solids, liquids or gases. Liquids and gases can be poured to fill a space. Liquids can make a surface wet. You cannot easily pass your hand through a solid. Many gases have no colour. Knowing these things helps us identify materials.

Science quiz

The table below tells you the properties of four different materials – chlorine, paraffin, mica and margarine.

Material	Chlorine	Paraffin	Mica	Margarine
Can it fill a space?	Yes	Yes	No	No
What colour is it?	Yellow	No colour	White and silvery	Yellow
Can it be poured?	Yes	Yes	No	No
Can you put your finger through it?	Yes	Yes	No	Yes
Can it make a piece of paper wet?	No	Yes	No	Yes

Which materials are solids? ....

Which materials are liquids? ....

Which materials are gases? ....

Science activity

Try putting drops of water, oil and washing-up liquid onto a mirror. Which liquid flows best? Which one sticks to the surface of the mirror best?

Does it become softer or harder?

Science facts

Some materials change when they are heated. If you heat liquid water to 100°C, it boils and changes into a gas called water vapour. When you heat solid butter or margarine, it melts and becomes liquid. Clay changes from a soft material into a hard material when it is heated to a very high temperature. When dough is heated in an oven, it changes into bread.

Science quiz

Use the words **softer** and **harder** to fill in the gaps and complete each of the sentences.

When you heat a potato in the oven, the inside becomes.........................

When you heat a raw egg, the inside becomes.........................

When you heat dough in an oven, the outside becomes.........................

When you cook food in a saucepan, the saucepan does not become

.... or ....

When you hold a bar of chocolate in your hand, it becomes.........................

Science activity

(!) Ask an adult to help you make toffee. Gently heat and dissolve 450 g of brown sugar in 150 ml of water. Slowly raise the heat to 130°C and then stir in 50 g of unsalted butter. Ask an adult to remove the mixture from the heat and pour it in a tin to cool. Describe the changes that take place.

Which materials feel warm?

Science facts

Some materials, such as metal, feel cold when you touch them because they draw the heat from your hand. They are said to be good thermal conductors. Others materials, such as wood, feel warm to the touch. They do not draw heat from your hand and are said to be good thermal insulators.

Science quiz

Five spoons made of different materials were placed in a bowl. Five people each held a spoon while hot water was poured into the bowl. When a spoon became too hot to hold, the holder let go and said "Now". Here are the results.

Type of spoon	How long it took to say "Now"
Plastic spoon	Did not say "Now"
Steel spoon	15 seconds
Wooden spoon	Did not say "Now"
China spoon	Did not say "Now"
Aluminium ladle	30 seconds

Science activity

(!) Put your hand inside a paper bag and pick up an ice cube. Try it again wearing a plastic bag on your hand. Do the same with an oven glove, a sock and a rubber glove. Which is the best thermal insulator?

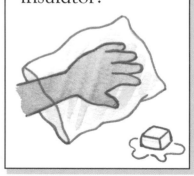

Which material is the best thermal conductor?

....

What happens when things cool?

Science facts

Some materials change when they are cooled. For example, liquid water changes into solid ice. Food becomes very hard when it is put in the freezer. Water vapour turns into liquid water when it cools, forming clouds of tiny water droplets in the air (steam) or droplets of condensation on cold windows.

Science quiz

Look at the picture below. Can you spot five examples of materials that have changed as they cooled? Draw a circle round each one.

Jelly

Science activity

(!) Take a packet of ice-cream mix and stir in water, as instructed on the packet. Pour the mixture into a polythene tub and put it in the freezer. When it starts to freeze, stir it quickly for about a minute. Put it back in the freezer until it is completely frozen. What changes take place when you make the ice cream?

Is the change reversible?

Science facts

When you heat solid ice, it changes into liquid water. If you then freeze the water, it changes back into solid ice. The change can go either way, so it is said to be reversible. When you heat soft clay in a kiln, it becomes very hard. But if you cool the clay, it will not change back to being soft. The change can only go one way, so it is said to be irreversible.

Science quiz

Which of these changes are reversible and which are irreversible?
In each case, circle the correct answer.

Paper burns to form ashes.

Reversible   Irreversible

Chocolate melts in your hand.

Reversible   Irreversible

Egg whites and sugar
cook to form meringues.

Reversible   Irreversible

Margarine melts when
it is spread on hot toast.

Reversible   Irreversible

Milk goes sour in
hot weather.

Reversible   Irreversible

Science activity

Mix 225 g of icing sugar, 170 g of desiccated coconut and 3 tablespoons of condensed milk. Spoon the mixture into a tin. Leave it for a day. You now have coconut ice! Are the changes that occur to the ingredients reversible?

How does the water cycle work?

Science facts

Evaporation is the process by which water (a liquid) turns into water vapour (a gas). Condensation is the process by which water vapour turns back into water. Evaporation is quickened by heating, and condensation is quickened by cooling. Water from seas, rivers and plants' leaves evaporates because of the Sun's heat. The water vapour gathers in the atmosphere. When this moisture-laden warm air meets colder air high in the atmosphere, it condenses to form clouds of tiny water droplets. When the droplets become big and heavy, they fall as rain. This rainwater soaks into the ground and eventually ends up back in rivers and seas.

Science quiz

Put a tick (✔) by the correct statements and a cross (✘) by the incorrect ones. Then decide whether or not statement 1 happens because of statement 2.

Statement 1	(✔) or (✘)	Statement 2	(✔) or (✘)	Statement 1 happens because of Statement 2 –True or False?
Rain falls when clouds are formed.		Water vapour condenses to form water when cooled.		
Water only evaporates from seas.		Water vapour is formed faster when water is warmed.		
Water vapour condenses faster in the higher regions of the atmosphere.		It is colder in the higher regions of the atmosphere.		

Science activity

Place a large, empty plastic bottle in a freezer for half an hour. Remove it and pour a quarter of a teaspoon of water into the bottle. Screw on the cap and leave it in a warm place for an hour. What do you notice? Place the bottle back in the freezer for half an hour. What do you notice now?

Will the bulb light up?

Science facts

A bulb will only light up if it is part of an electric circuit. A circuit is a complete path around which electricity can flow. It must include a source of electricity, such as a battery. To make the circuit, the bulb is connected to the battery by wires. Electricity flows out of the battery, around the circuit and back into the battery. The bulb lights up when electricity passes through it.

Science quiz

Sarah made a bulb light up by connecting these parts together to make an electric circuit. Can you draw the circuit she made?

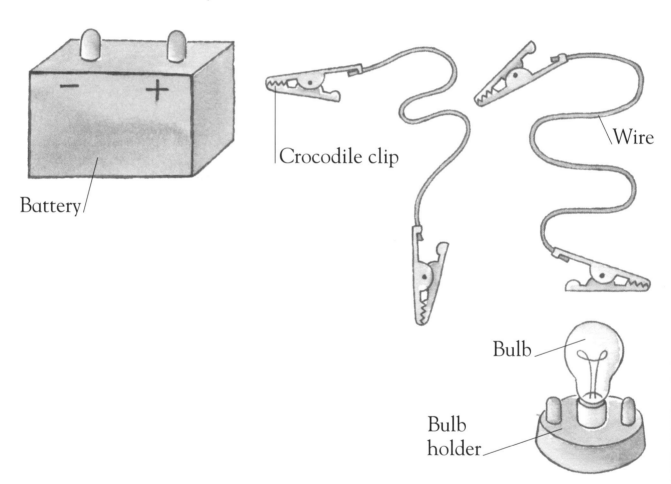

Battery

Crocodile clip

Wire

Bulb

Bulb holder

Science activity

(!) Can you make two bulbs light up at once? You will need to build a circuit using a battery, two bulbs in bulb holders and at least three connecting wires.

Will it switch on and off?

Science facts

A switch allows a circuit to be turned on and off. The switch can close a gap to complete a circuit so that electricity can flow through it. It can also open a gap to break the circuit and stop electricity flowing. You can put a switch anywhere in a circuit.

Science quiz

On the right is a simple switch. To make it work, you push down on the metal strip until it touches the connecting pin to complete the circuit. Look at the circuit diagrams below. Is the bulb on or off in each one? Circle the correct answer.

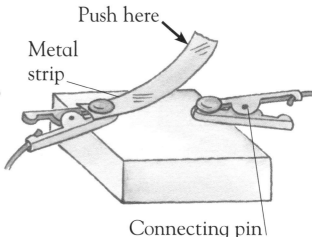

Push here

Metal strip

Connecting pin

Key to diagrams

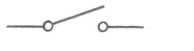

Open switch

Closed switch

Bulb

Battery

Wire

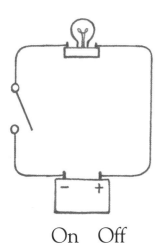

On   Off

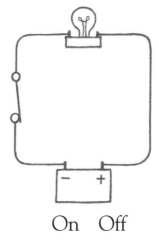

On   Off

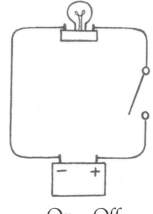

On   Off

On   Off

Science activity

(!) Build a circuit using a battery, a bulb and some connecting wires. Try making a switch. Use a piece of balsa wood, two drawing pins and a strip of aluminium foil. Connect your switch to the circuit.

Will it conduct electricity?

Science facts

When you build an electric circuit, all the parts of the circuit must be connected. Each part must also let electricity flow through it before the circuit will work. Materials that allow electricity to flow through them are called electrical conductors. Materials that do not let electricity flow through them are called electrical insulators.

Science quiz

Which of the objects below will make the buzzer sound when they are connected to the crocodile clips in the circuit? Put a tick (✔) beside each one that makes the buzzer sound.

☐ PVC-coated wire not stripped at the ends

☐ PVC-coated wire stripped at the ends

☐ Spaghetti

☐ String

☐ Nylon fishing line

☐ Iron wire

☐ Paper

☐ Wooden rod

Crocodile clips

4.5-volt battery

Wire connectors

Buzzer

Object being tested

Science activity

(!) Look closely at a light bulb like the one shown below (look at one that is not connected to a bulb holder or a socket). Can you work out how electricity travels through the bulb? How does the bulb connect to a circuit?

What makes the sound?

Science facts

Sounds are made when objects vibrate. We say that an object vibrates when it moves rapidly to and fro. If you hold a ruler on the edge of a table and twang it, the ruler vibrates and makes a sound. All musical instruments have parts that vibrate to make sound. A recorder, for example, contains a column of air that vibrates when you blow into the instrument.

Science quiz

Here are some pictures of musical instruments. Draw a cross on the part of each instrument that vibrates to make the sound.

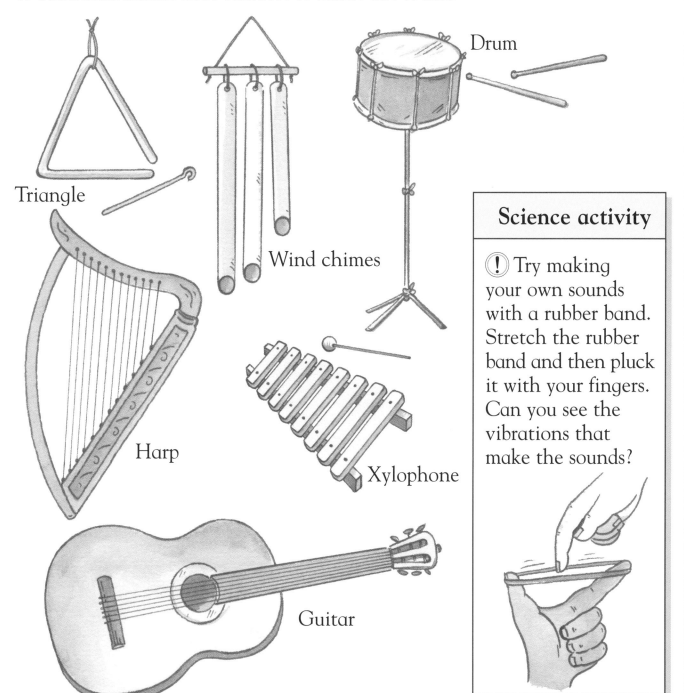

Triangle

Wind chimes

Drum

Harp

Xylophone

Guitar

Science activity

(!) Try making your own sounds with a rubber band. Stretch the rubber band and then pluck it with your fingers. Can you see the vibrations that make the sounds?

How are sounds changed?

Science facts

The faster an object vibrates, the higher the sound it makes. The slower an object vibrates, the lower the sound it makes. The speed at which a guitar string, drum skin or column of air in a recorder vibrates is called its pitch. Musical instruments have a high pitch or a low pitch.

Science quiz

Look at these musical instruments. Draw a line from each instrument to the way you change its pitch.

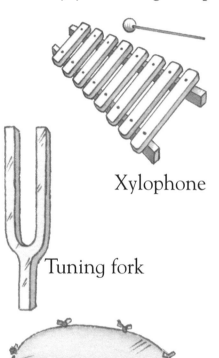

Xylophone

Tuning fork

Drum

Make its strings
longer or shorter.

Make the column of
air longer or shorter.

Increase or
reduce its size.

Change the size of
its wooden bars.

Make its skin
tighter or slacker.

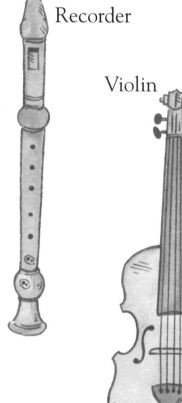

Recorder

Violin

Science activity

Hold a ruler on the edge of a table and twang it to make it vibrate. What sound do you get when only a little of the ruler sticks out over the table edge? What sound do you get when a lot of the ruler sticks out over the edge?

What makes sound louder?

Science facts

If you hit a cymbal softly, it makes a quiet sound. If you hit it hard, it makes a loud sound. The harder you pluck a guitar string, the louder the sound it makes. The harder you blow a whistle, the louder the sound it makes. All musical instruments work in the same way.

Science quiz

Earl put some grains of rice on the skin of a tambourine. When he beat the tambourine, the rice jumped up and down as the skin vibrated.

What do you think happened to the rice grains when Earl beat the tambourine harder?

....

Science activity

You can make a simple instrument called a kazoo by folding tissue paper over the teeth of a comb. To play the kazoo, you press it to your mouth and hum through it with pursed lips. How can you make the kazoo produce a louder sound?

How does sound travel?

Science facts

When a person sings, the vocal cords in the throat make the air vibrate. These vibrations travel through the air to your ears. You hear the vibrating air as sounds. Try feeling the vibrations in your throat when you sing. Sound can only travel as vibrations.

Science quiz

Here are two children using a string telephone. The sentences below explain how the boy can hear the girl speak, but they are jumbled up. Write the numbers 1 to 5 in the boxes to show what the correct order should be.

☐ The string vibrates.

☐ The vibrations are heard by the ear.

☐ The girl's vocal cords vibrate.

☐ The air vibrates in the girl's yogurt pot.

☐ The air vibrates in the boy's yogurt pot.

Science activity

(!) Can you make a spaghetti telephone? Use two yogurt pots and some long strands of dry spaghetti to connect them. Ask an adult to help you make a small hole in the base of each pot to insert the spaghetti. Be careful, as spaghetti breaks easily.

Answer Section with Parents' Notes
Key Stage 2
Ages 8–9

This section provides answers and explanatory notes to the quizzes and activities in the book. Work through each page together and ensure that your child understands each task. Point out any mistakes in your child's work and correct any errors, but also remember to praise your child's efforts and achievements. Where appropriate, ask your child to predict the outcome of the *Science activity* experiments. After each experiment, challenge your child to explain the results.

(!) If a *Science activity* box includes this caution symbol, extra care is necessary. In such cases, experiments may involve heavy weights, sharp objects, hot water, ice or soil. Always wear gloves when handling soil and ensure hands are washed afterwards. Gloves are also advisable for activities in which hot or very cold objects are used.

---

2 ☆ ## Is it an animal or a plant?

Science facts
Plants and animals are living things. Animals usually move from place to place to find food. Animals are sensitive to their surroundings and usually respond quickly to changes. Plants are green and usually rooted to the ground. They do not need to move to feed because they make their own food. Plants respond to light by growing towards its source.

Science quiz
These living things look very much alike. Write the letter **P** in the boxes beside the ones you think are plants. Write the letter **A** in the boxes beside the ones you think are animals.

A sea anemone captures food with its tentacles. It moves slowly. **A**

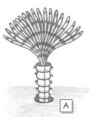
A peacock worm moves up and down in its tube and catches food with its tentacles. **A**

A liverwort makes its own food and does not move. **P**

A feather star uses its arms to move from place to place to find food. **A**

Moss is green and makes its own food. **P**

Science activity
(!) Germinate some mung beans. When the bean seedlings develop their first leaves, place them in a shoebox. Put the lid on the box. Ask an adult to cut a slit on one side, so that light can get in. What do you think the seedlings will look like after a few days?

The key difference between plants and animals is that plants are able to make their own food by a process called photosynthesis, which requires light. The seedlings in the *Science activity* will bend over as they try to grow towards the light.

---

3 ## What kind of animal is it? ☆

Science facts
It is easy to see how one animal is different from another. It is more difficult to say how animals are alike. We can put animals into groups according to the features they have in common. For example, animals that can keep their body warm, lay eggs, do not have teeth, have feathers on their body and scales on their legs belong to the group of animals we call birds.

Science quiz
What features do the animals in each group have in common? What is the name of each group of animals?

Common features of group A animals:
They have fur or hair.
They feed their young with milk.

These animals are __mammals.__

Rabbit
A
Human
Cow
Badger

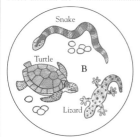
Snake
Turtle
B
Lizard

Common features of group B animals:
They have scaly skin.
They lay eggs.

These animals are __reptiles.__

Science activity

Collect together as many different kinds of coin as you can. Sort them into groups. What features do the coins in each group have in common?

This page introduces your child to the idea of different animal groups. Your child will begin to understand that we classify animals so that we can identify them more easily. Discuss how the missing groups – fish and amphibians – might be described.

---

4 ☆ ## What kind of plant is it?

Science facts
It is easy to see how one plant is different from another. It is more difficult to say how plants are alike. We can put plants into groups according to the features they have in common. For example, the plants we call mosses produce spores, have green bodies that often look like leaves and have thin parts to hold the plants in the soil.

Science quiz
What features do the plants in each group have in common? What is the name of each group of plants?

Cypress
Fir
A
Pine

Common features of group A plants:
They have cones.
They have straight leaves.

These plants are __conifers.__

Common features of group B plants:
They have flowers.
They have flat, veined leaves.

These plants are __flowering plants.__

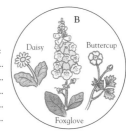
B
Daisy
Buttercup
Foxglove

Science activity

Compare two different types of flower. Write down as many ways as you can in which they are different and as many ways as you can in which they are the same.

Your child will learn about different plant groups. Differences in plants are easier for children to spot than similarities. Flower similarities might be that they all have petals, pollen-carrying parts (stamens) and a single piece in the middle (the carpel).

Are you an animal detective?

Science facts

An animal key helps you identify different animals. If you don't know an animal's name, a key will give you all the clues you need. Solve the clues one by one and you will discover the name of the animal, just like a detective solving a mystery.

Science quiz

Follow this Yes/No animal key to find the names of the insects in the pictures.

Clue 1 Does the insect have very large eyes? If yes, go to clue 2.
Does the insect have small eyes? If yes, go to clue 3.

Clue 2 Are the insect's eyes touching? If yes, it is a dragonfly.
If the insect's eyes are not touching, it is a damselfly.

Clue 3 Does the head have a long pointed beak? If yes, it is a scorpion fly.
If the head does not have a pointed beak, go to clue 4.

Clue 4 Does the insect have three tails? If yes, it is a mayfly.
Does the insect have only one tail? If yes, it is a lacewing.

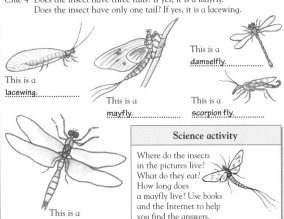

This is a <u>damselfly.</u>

This is a <u>lacewing.</u>

This is a <u>mayfly.</u>

This is a <u>scorpion fly.</u>

This is a <u>dragonfly.</u>

Science activity

Where do the insects in the pictures live? What do they eat? How long does a mayfly live? Use books and the Internet to help you find the answers.

Children will need help to use the Yes/No key, but they will find it rewarding to identify the insects. Assist your child to research these insects, using reference books and the Internet (there are plenty of good animal websites for kids).

Are you a plant detective?

Science facts

By using a plant key, you can become a plant detective and discover the names of different plants. A plant key gives you all the clues you need to identify a plant. The key shown below is called a branching key. If you follow the branch that describes what you see, it will lead you to the plant's name.

Science quiz

Use this branching Yes/No key to find the names of these fruits.

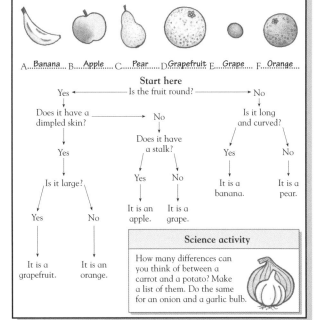

A. <u>Banana</u> B. <u>Apple</u> C. <u>Pear</u> D. <u>Grapefruit</u> E. <u>Grape</u> F. <u>Orange</u>

Start here

Is the fruit round?

Yes ← → No

Does it have a dimpled skin? → No

Is it long and curved?

Yes ↓

Is it large?

Does it have a stalk?

Yes / No

It is an apple. It is a grape.

Yes → It is a banana.

No → It is a pear.

Yes / No

It is a grapefruit. It is an orange.

Science activity

How many differences can you think of between a carrot and a potato? Make a list of them. Do the same for an onion and a garlic bulb.

Here, your child learns how to use another kind of Yes/No key. To use it, answer the questions with a yes or no and then follow the lines until you come to the next question or the answer. Talk your child through this procedure before starting.

What happens when things die?

Science facts

Animals such as earthworms feed on dead plants. Other animals, such as maggots, feed on dead animals. There are also tiny living things called micro-organisms that feed on dead animals and plants. Bacteria and many types of fungus are micro-organisms. They cause dead things to decay.

Science quiz

Here are some animals found in woodlands, where there are decaying leaves. Can you use this Yes/No key to find their names?

Clue 1 Does the animal have six legs? If yes, it is a springtail.
Does the animal have more than six legs? If yes, go to clue 2.

Clue 2 Does it have eight legs? If yes, it is a harvestman.
Does it have more than eight legs? If yes, go to clue 3.

Clue 3 Does it have a broad, flat body? If yes, it is a woodlouse.
Does it have a long, thin body? If yes, go to clue 4.

Clue 4 Does each section of the body have two legs? If yes, it is a centipede.
Does each section of the body have four legs? If yes, it is a millipede.

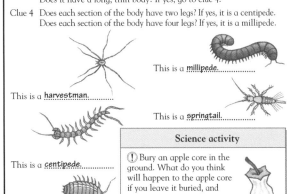

This is a <u>millipede.</u>

This is a <u>harvestman.</u>

This is a <u>springtail.</u>

This is a <u>centipede.</u>

This is a <u>woodlouse.</u>

Science activity

(!) Bury an apple core in the ground. What do you think will happen to the apple core if you leave it buried, and why? Dig up the core after three weeks to see whether your prediction is correct.

Dead animals and plants provide food for a range of living things that decompose the remains. In the food chain, these organisms are called reducers. Reducers are important, as they recycle nutrients such as carbon, nitrogen and minerals.

What animal lives where?

Science facts

Animals come in many different shapes and sizes. Most animals live in one type of habitat because they are suited to it. They are adapted to suit the environment in which they live. For example, many frogs, newts and toads have webbed feet to help them swim in their watery habitat. Squirrels have sharp claws to grip and long tails to help them balance as they scramble up and down trees.

Science quiz

Look at these pictures. Explain how each animal is adapted to its habitat.

A desert fox lives in hot, dry places. <u>Short fur keeps it cool; its large ears help it lose heat.</u>

A mole burrows in dark underground tunnels. <u>Long claws help it dig; eyes are tiny, as it doesn't need to see in the dark.</u>

An arctic fox lives in cold places. <u>Long fur keeps it warm; small ears prevent heat loss.</u>

A dormouse is active at night. It climbs shrubs and trees. <u>Large eyes help it see at night; a long tail helps it balance.</u>

Science activity

Can you find some animals in your garden or local park? Make a list of the animals and the places where you found them. Write some notes about the ways in which each animal is suited to where it lives.

Use the opportunity of exploring the garden to discuss how animals are adapted to suit their particular lifestyles. For example, worms have no legs so they can burrow easily and hedgehogs have spines for protection against predators.

What plant lives where?

Science facts

Plants are suited, or adapted, to the different habitats in which they grow. Those growing on land usually have stiff stems to hold them upright, while water plants tend to have weaker stems because the water supports them. Plants in hot, dry places often have short or few leaves so that they do not lose too much water. Some also store water in thick stems. Plants growing in shaded areas often have large leaves to trap as much sunlight as possible.

Science quiz

Look at the drawings below. Explain how each plant is suited to its habitat.

 A cactus growing in a hot, dry area.

Its stem stores water; its leaves have become spines
to stop water loss.

Pond weed growing just under the surface of water.

It has a weak stem as the water supports it.

A daisy growing in mowed or grazed grass.

It grows close to the ground to survive mowing or grazing.

Look at these two dandelion plants. Which one do you think grew underneath a tree? Why?

The dandelion with the bigger leaf grew under a tree.

It needed a bigger leaf to get enough light.

Science activity

⚠ Explore some woodland or shaded parts of a garden with an adult. Can you find any difference between plants such as dandelions and nettles growing under bushes or trees and those growing in open areas?

Plants are also adapted to suit their particular habitats. Encourage your child to look at local plants and to try and work out ways in which they are adapted to living there. Praise any comment that shows thought and understanding.

How do we affect living things?

Science facts

The activities of humans can affect the lives of animals and plants. Pollution from factories and cars can poison the air and water that animals and plants need to survive. The places where they feed and reproduce are often used to build houses and shops. Humans need places to live and work, but there must be a balance between human needs and the needs of animals and plants.

Science quiz

Draw a circle around each thing in this picture that could cause harm to animals and plants.

Science activity

Put a clean piece of white paper outside. It should be in the open air but in a place that is sheltered from the rain. Put a mug on top of the paper. What do you think the paper will look like after a week? What will you find when you lift up the mug?

Discuss environmental issues in a balanced way. Explain why farmers spray crops and the need to build factories to provide jobs and houses for people to live in. Explain also how these activities affect the environment and living things within it.

What is the digestive system?

Science facts

The digestive system turns food into nutrients that our bodies need to survive.

Science quiz

Use the words in the box to complete the sentences.

Oesophagus   Large intestine   Mouth   Small intestine   Stomach

Mouth

Oesophagus

Stomach

Small intestine

Large intestine

1 The digestion process begins in the ___mouth___ , where food is chewed and mixed with saliva.

2 The ___oesophagus___ connects the mouth to the stomach.

3 The ___stomach___ contains an acid fluid that breaks down food.

4 The ___small intestine___ is a long tube where nutrients from digested food pass into the bloodstream.

5 The ___large intestine___ absorbs water from food and turns the parts of food that you can't digest into waste.

The small intestine can grow to more than 6 metres long and folds over many times so it will fit in the human body. As food makes the long journey through the intestines, the body absorbs nutrients through the intestinal walls.

What do our teeth do?

Science facts

Humans have four different types of tooth. Young children have about 20 teeth, called milk teeth. They have eight teeth called incisors at the front of the mouth (four above and four below). These are used for cutting food. The next four sharp, pointed teeth are the canines, which are used for tearing food. Next to these are the premolars, used for grinding and chewing. Between the ages of five and ten years, these milk teeth are replaced by adult ones, which include another twelve teeth called molars. These are also used for chewing.

Science quiz

Animals that eat meat have sharp, pointed teeth called canines and scissor-like teeth called premolars and molars to cut and tear meat. Animals that eat plants have large, flat molars for grinding and chewing. Humans eat both meat and plants. What sort of teeth do humans have? Label each type of tooth shown in the diagram below.

Incisor

Upper jaw

Molar

Canine

Lower jaw

A set of adult human teeth

Science activity

Use a mirror to look inside your own mouth. Then, in the diagram above, colour in all the teeth that you have. You may not have all the teeth in the diagram as it shows an adult's teeth. Check with your friends and some adults to see if they have the same number of teeth as you.

Your child will learn that humans have four types of tooth, each of which has a different function. Show your child your molars (he or she may not yet have any) and encourage him or her to consider the purpose of teeth while eating food.

What causes tooth decay?

Science facts

When we chew food, some of it becomes stuck between our teeth. Tiny living things in our mouths, called bacteria, attack this food and feed on it themselves. As the bacteria feed, they produce acid, which can decay our teeth. By cleaning our teeth after meals, the bits of food are brushed away so the bacteria cannot feed and produce acid.

Science quiz

A class of children were expecting to see the school dentist. Their teacher asked them to do a survey of how often they cleaned their teeth. The block graph below shows the results of their survey.

How often we clean our teeth

Never						
Not very often	Sean	Sam				
Sometimes	James	Amy				
Most days	Oliver	Aziz	Emily	Maria		
Twice each day	Mina	John	Ling	Emma	Earl	Rachel

Which children are most likely to need treatment from the dentist?
Sean and Sam

Science activity

Which is the best way of cleaning your teeth: eating an apple, rinsing with water or brushing then rinsing? Ask an adult to help you use disclosing tablets to test the three ways of cleaning. (Disclosing tablets reveal bacteria in the mouth.)

Chewing a disclosing tablet is a good way to test the effectiveness of brushing habits, because it colours bacteria red. Avoiding sugary foods will limit the growth of bacteria in the mouth, while alkaline toothpaste will help neutralise acids.

Are animal teeth the same as ours?

Science facts

You have different teeth for doing different jobs. The sharp front teeth, called incisors, bite and cut up food. The flat back teeth, called molars, grind up food before it is swallowed. You also have pointed teeth near the front of your mouth that grip, pierce and tear food. These are called canines. Animals such as tigers and lions have large canines to catch and kill their prey.

Science quiz

An animal's skull clearly shows its teeth. Look at the teeth on the rabbit skull and the cat skull below.

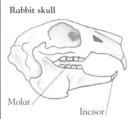

Rabbit skull — Molar — Incisor

Cat skull — Incisor — Molar — Canine

Why does the rabbit have large incisors?
To cut up the grass it eats.

Why doesn't the rabbit have canines?
It does not kill other animals.

How can you tell that the cat catches and eats other animals?
It has large canines.

Why does the cat have such small incisors?
It does not use them to cut up food.

Science activity

Using a small mirror, count how many teeth you have. How many of each type are there? Do you have teeth like a meat-eating carnivore or a plant-eating herbivore?

Your child will count 8 to 12 molars, 8 premolars, 4 canines and 8 incisors (give or take a few that haven't yet grown or have been removed). This shows that humans are both herbivores and carnivores – in other words, we are omnivores.

Is it a food chain?

Science facts

Plants and seaweeds can make their own food. They are called producers. Herbivores eat plants to obtain proteins, carbohydrates and fats. They use these nutrients to grow and for energy. Carnivores eat herbivores and use the meat in the same way. Carnivores are called predators and the animals they eat are called prey. There is a chain from plants, to herbivores that eat plants, to carnivores that eat herbivores. This is called a food chain.

Science quiz

Look at the pictures and find the animals or plants that complete these food chains. Write their names in the spaces on the chart.

Plant makes food	Herbivore eats plant	Carnivore eats herbivore
Pansy	_Slug_	Thrush
Seaweed	Periwinkle	_Seagull_
Oak leaf	Caterpillar	Robin
Grass	_Cow_	_Human_

Seagull — Slug — Oak leaf — Human — Cow

Science activity

Many birds are herbivores, but some are carnivores. Draw and label a food chain that includes a bird as a herbivore. Draw another chain showing a bird as a carnivore.

In food chains, plants are called producers (they produce food for the rest of the chain). Herbivores, which eat plants, are called first consumers. Carnivores are second consumers. Carnivores that eat other carnivores are third consumers.

What is a food chain?

Science facts

A food chain is the feeding relationship between different plants and animals in a particular environment, or habitat. A plant is nearly always at the start of a food chain because it produces food. It is called a producer. Consumers are animals that eat producers or other consumers. The animal in a food chain that eats the producer is called the first consumer. The animal that eats the first consumer is called the second consumer, and so on. The direction of arrows between the organisms in a food chain shows what is eaten by what.

Producer — First consumer — Second consumer — Third consumer

Science quiz

Look at the two food chains below. Identify the producer, first consumer and second consumer in each food chain. Write your answers in the table.

A Plant plankton → Water flea → Stickleback → Dragonfly larva → Pike

B Water plant → Water snails → Water-beetle larva → Frog → Heron

Food chain	Producer	First consumer	Second consumer
A	_Plant plankton_	_Water flea_	_Stickleback_
B	_Water plant_	_Water snails_	_Water-beetle larva_

Science activity

Write these words on some cards: **Plant material**, **Carp** (a fish that feeds on plant material), **Heron** (a bird that feeds on fish) and **Pike** (a fish that feeds on other fish). Now make a food chain by placing the cards in order and by putting some arrow cards in the correct direction between them.

Your child will learn how to make a food chain and to identify producers and first and second consumers in a chain. You may wish to explain to your child that the pike and heron in the food chains in the *Science quiz* are fourth consumers.

Is it solid?

Science facts
Materials are either solids, liquids or gases. You can recognise solid materials by their properties. Solids do not change shape by themselves and you cannot push your finger through them easily. Solids do not make things wet.

Science quiz
Look at the materials below. Put a tick (✔) beside each one that you think is a solid.
Hint: for materials such as sand and salt, think about the individual grains.

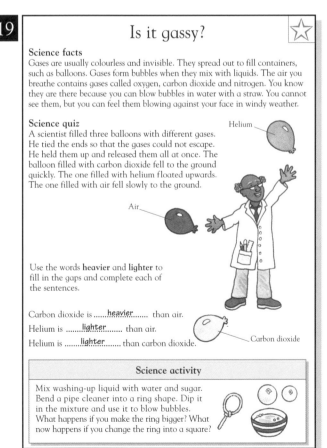

Modelling clay ✔
Aluminium kitchen foil ✔
Wood ✔
Sand ✔
Salt ✔
Marbles ✔

Science activity
(!) Whisk the white of an egg until it becomes stiff. What happens if you leave it for a while? When you boil an egg, the egg white becomes solid. What happens if you leave the egg white for a while?

Solids are made up of submicroscopic particles that are packed closely together. All the materials in the picture are solids. Although you can push your finger through a pile of salt or sand and you can pour them, the individual grains are still solid.

How runny is it?

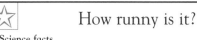

Science facts
Liquids are materials that make things wet. All liquids flow. This means that they are runny and you can pour them. If you spill liquids, they spread out. A liquid will fill a container, such as a bottle. If you leave a liquid to stand, its surface will become level. You can easily push your finger through a liquid.

Science quiz
A class of children did an experiment to find out which of the five liquids below was the runniest. The same amount of each liquid was poured from a jug into a glass. The time it took to fill each glass was written down.

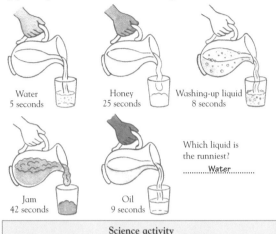

Water 5 seconds
Honey 25 seconds
Washing-up liquid 8 seconds
Jam 42 seconds
Oil 9 seconds

Which liquid is the runniest?
............Water

Science activity
If you drop a marble into a glass of honey and another into a glass of treacle at the same time, which one will reach the bottom first? Which liquid is runnier?

The submicroscopic particles in liquids are farther apart than those in solids, which is why liquids are able to flow. Try the *Science activity* using other liquids, such as washing-up liquid and cooking oil, or water and glycerine.

Is it gassy?

Science facts
Gases are usually colourless and invisible. They spread out to fill containers, such as balloons. Gases form bubbles when they mix with liquids. The air you breathe contains gases called oxygen, carbon dioxide and nitrogen. You know they are there because you can blow bubbles in water with a straw. You cannot see them, but you can feel them blowing against your face in windy weather.

Science quiz
A scientist filled three balloons with different gases. He tied the ends so that the gases could not escape. He held them up and released them all at once. The balloon filled with carbon dioxide fell to the ground quickly. The one filled with helium floated upwards. The one filled with air fell slowly to the ground.

Helium
Air
Carbon dioxide

Use the words **heavier** and **lighter** to fill in the gaps and complete each of the sentences.

Carbon dioxide is ......heavier....... than air.
Helium is ......lighter....... than air.
Helium is ......lighter....... than carbon dioxide.

Science activity
Mix washing-up liquid with water and sugar. Bend a pipe cleaner into a ring shape. Dip it in the mixture and use it to blow bubbles. What happens if you make the ring bigger? What now happens if you change the ring into a square?

The submicroscopic particles in gases are very far apart, so your hand passes easily through them. In the *Science activity*, the bigger the ring, the bigger the bubbles. The bubbles will always be spherical, unless the pipe-cleaner "ring" is cube-shaped.

What kind of material is it?

Science facts
Materials can exist as solids, liquids or gases. Liquids and gases can be poured to fill a space. Liquids can make a surface wet. You cannot easily pass your hand through a solid. Many gases have no colour. Knowing these things helps us identify materials.

Science quiz
The table below tells you the properties of four different materials – chlorine, paraffin, mica and margarine.

Material	Chlorine	Paraffin	Mica	Margarine
Can it fill a space?	Yes	Yes	No	No
What colour is it?	Yellow	No colour	White and silvery	Yellow
Can it be poured?	Yes	Yes	No	No
Can you put your finger through it?	Yes	Yes	No	Yes
Can it make a piece of paper wet?	No	Yes	No	Yes

Which materials are solids? Mica and margarine
Which materials are liquids? Paraffin
Which materials are gases? Chlorine

Science activity
Try putting drops of water, oil and washing-up liquid onto a mirror. Which liquid flows best? Which one sticks to the surface of the mirror best?

Your child will learn to distinguish between solids, liquids and gases. Chlorine is an unusual gas, because it is coloured. Mica is a solid mineral. The *Science activity* shows that most liquids will stick to a surface, but some are stickier than others.

Does it become softer or harder?

Science facts
Some materials change when they are heated. If you heat liquid water to 100°C, it boils and changes into a gas called water vapour. When you heat solid butter or margarine, it melts and becomes liquid. Clay changes from a soft material into a hard material when it is heated to a very high temperature. When dough is heated in an oven, it changes into bread.

Science quiz
Use the words **softer** and **harder** to fill in the gaps and complete each of the sentences.

When you heat a potato in the oven, the inside becomes .softer.

When you heat a raw egg, the inside becomes .harder.

When you heat dough in an oven, the outside becomes .harder.

When you cook food in a saucepan, the saucepan does not become .softer. or .harder.

When you hold a bar of chocolate in your hand, it becomes .softer.

Science activity

(!) Ask an adult to help you make toffee. Gently heat and dissolve 450 g of brown sugar in 150 ml of water. Slowly raise the heat to 130°C and then stir in 50 g of unsalted butter. Ask an adult to remove the mixture from the heat and pour it in a tin to cool. Describe the changes that take place.

Your child will learn that some materials change when they are heated. A metal saucepan does not change during cooking, but if heated to very high temperatures it will eventually melt. You should supervise your child for the toffee-making activity.

Which materials feel warm?

Science facts
Some materials, such as metal, feel cold when you touch them because they draw the heat from your hand. They are said to be good thermal conductors. Others materials, such as wood, feel warm to the touch. They do not draw heat from your hand and are said to be good thermal insulators.

Science quiz
Five spoons made of different materials were placed in a bowl. Five people each held a spoon while hot water was poured into the bowl. When a spoon became too hot to hold, the holder let go and said "Now". Here are the results.

Type of spoon	How long it took to say "Now"
Plastic spoon	Did not say "Now"
Steel spoon	15 seconds
Wooden spoon	Did not say "Now"
China spoon	Did not say "Now"
Aluminium ladle	30 seconds

Science activity

(!) Put your hand inside a paper bag and pick up an ice cube. Try it again wearing a plastic bag on your hand. Do the same with an oven glove, a sock and a rubber glove. Which is the best thermal insulator?

Which material is the best thermal conductor?
.... Steel ....

Metals are good thermal conductors, but some, such as steel, are better than others, such as aluminium. In the *Science activity*, the oven glove is the best insulator, because air (a poor thermal conductor) gets trapped in tiny spaces inside the material.

What happens when things cool?

Science facts
Some materials change when they are cooled. For example, liquid water changes into solid ice. Food becomes very hard when it is put in the freezer. Water vapour turns into liquid water when it cools, forming clouds of tiny water droplets in the air (steam) or droplets of condensation on cold windows.

Science quiz
Look at the picture below. Can you spot five examples of materials that have changed as they cooled? Draw a circle round each one.

Jelly

Science activity

(!) Take a packet of ice-cream mix and stir in water, as instructed on the packet. Pour the mixture into a polythene tub and put it in the freezer. When it starts to freeze, stir it quickly for about a minute. Put it back in the freezer until it is completely frozen. What changes take place when you make the ice cream?

Water vapour (a gas) rising from a saucepan cools to form steam (tiny, liquid water droplets suspended in the air). Water vapour in the air condenses into liquid water on cold surfaces. Liquid water turns to ice in the freezer. Liquid jelly sets as it cools.

Is the change reversible?

Science facts
When you heat solid ice, it changes into liquid water. If you then freeze the water, it changes back into solid ice. The change can go either way, so it is said to be reversible. When you heat soft clay in a kiln, it becomes very hard. But if you cool the clay, it will not change back to being soft. The change can only go one way, so it is said to be irreversible.

Science quiz
Which of these changes are reversible and which are irreversible? In each case, circle the correct answer.

Paper burns to form ashes.
Reversible (Irreversible)

Chocolate melts in your hand.
(Reversible) Irreversible

Egg whites and sugar cook to form meringues.
Reversible (Irreversible)

Margarine melts when it is spread on hot toast.
(Reversible) Irreversible

Milk goes sour in hot weather.
Reversible (Irreversible)

Science activity

Mix 225 g of icing sugar, 170 g of desiccated coconut and 3 tablespoons of condensed milk. Spoon the mixture into a tin. Leave it for a day. You now have coconut ice! Are the changes that occur to the ingredients reversible?

Melting is a physical change that can be reversed by lowering the temperature. Burning, cooking and the souring of milk are irreversible, because a chemical change has taken place. The coconut's change in the *Science activity* is irreversible.

How does the water cycle work?

Science facts

Evaporation is the process by which water (a liquid) turns into water vapour (a gas). Condensation is the process by which water vapour turns back into water. Evaporation is quickened by heating, and condensation is quickened by cooling. Water from seas, rivers and plants' leaves evaporates because of the Sun's heat. The water vapour gathers in the atmosphere. When this moisture-laden warm air meets colder air high in the atmosphere, it condenses to form clouds of tiny water droplets. When the droplets become big and heavy, they fall as rain. This rainwater soaks into the ground and eventually ends up back in rivers and seas.

Science quiz

Put a tick (✔) by the correct statements and a cross (✘) by the incorrect ones. Then decide whether or not statement 1 happens because of statement 2.

Statement 1	(✔) or (✘)	Statement 2	(✔) or (✘)	Statement 1 happens because of Statement 2 – True or False?
Rain falls when clouds are formed.	✘	Water vapour condenses to form water when cooled.	✔	False
Water only evaporates from seas.	✘	Water vapour is formed faster when water is warmed.	✔	False
Water vapour condenses faster in the higher regions of the atmosphere.	✔	It is colder in the higher regions of the atmosphere.	✔	True

Science activity

Place a large, empty plastic bottle in a freezer for half an hour. Remove it and pour a quarter of a teaspoon of water into the bottle. Screw on the cap and leave it in a warm place for an hour. What do you notice? Place the bottle back in the freezer for half an hour. What do you notice now?

In the *Science activity*, help your child predict that the bottled water will disappear when put in a warm place and will return when the bottle cools. If this doesn't happen, repeat the activity using a smaller quantity of water and warmer conditions.

Will the bulb light up?

Science facts

A bulb will only light up if it is part of an electric circuit. A circuit is a complete path around which electricity can flow. It must include a source of electricity, such as a battery. To make the circuit, the bulb is connected to the battery by wires. Electricity flows out of the battery, around the circuit and back into the battery. The bulb lights up when electricity passes through it.

Science quiz

Sarah made a bulb light up by connecting these parts together to make an electric circuit. Can you draw the circuit she made?

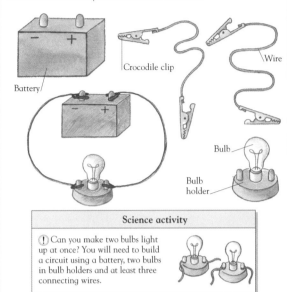

Crocodile clip · Wire · Battery · Bulb · Bulb holder

Science activity

(!) Can you make two bulbs light up at once? You will need to build a circuit using a battery, two bulbs in bulb holders and at least three connecting wires.

Your child will learn that a complete circuit is needed before a bulb or other component can work. For the *Science activity*, you will need to provide a 4.5-V battery, two 4.5-V-rated bulbs (or festoon lamps) in holders and wires with crocodile clips.

Will it switch on and off?

Science facts

A switch allows a circuit to be turned on and off. The switch can close a gap to complete a circuit so that electricity can flow through it. It can also open a gap to break the circuit and stop electricity flowing. You can put a switch anywhere in a circuit.

Science quiz

On the right is a simple switch. To make it work, you push down on the metal strip until it touches the connecting pin to complete the circuit. Look at the circuit diagrams below. Is the bulb on or off in each one? Circle the correct answer.

Push here · Metal strip · Connecting pin

Key to diagrams

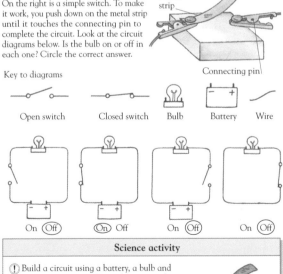

Open switch · Closed switch · Bulb · Battery · Wire

On **(Off)** · **(On)** Off · On **(Off)** · On **(Off)**

Science activity

(!) Build a circuit using a battery, a bulb and some connecting wires. Try making a switch. Use a piece of balsa wood, two drawing pins and a strip of aluminium foil. Connect your switch to the circuit.

Your child will learn that a switch can be used to control a circuit. There are a variety of switches, including toggle, push and knife switches, but they all work in the same way, closing or opening a gap in the circuit to turn it on or off.

Will it conduct electricity?

Science facts

When you build an electric circuit, all the parts of the circuit must be connected. Each part must also let electricity flow through it before the circuit will work. Materials that allow electricity to flow through them are called electrical conductors. Materials that do not let electricity flow through them are called electrical insulators.

Science quiz

Which of the objects below will make the buzzer sound when they are connected to the crocodile clips in the circuit? Put a tick (✔) beside each one that makes the buzzer sound.

- [ ] PVC-coated wire not stripped at the ends
- [ ] Nylon fishing line
- [✔] PVC-coated wire stripped at the ends
- [✔] Iron wire
- [ ] Spaghetti
- [ ] Paper
- [ ] String
- [ ] Wooden rod

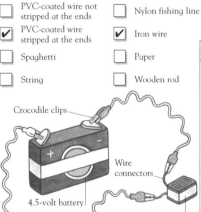

Crocodile clips · Wire connectors · 4.5-volt battery · Buzzer · Object being tested

Science activity

(!) Look closely at a light bulb like the one shown below (look at one that is not connected to a bulb holder or a socket). Can you work out how electricity travels through the bulb? How does the bulb connect to a circuit?

Only metals and a few other materials, such as carbon, conduct electricity. If your child can build this circuit, he or she will have a metal detector. Your child can predict if a material is metal and then test the prediction with the metal detector.

What makes the sound?

Science facts

Sounds are made when objects vibrate. We say that an object vibrates when it moves rapidly to and fro. If you hold a ruler on the edge of a table and twang it, the ruler vibrates and makes a sound. All musical instruments have parts that vibrate to make sound. A recorder, for example, contains a column of air that vibrates when you blow into the instrument.

Science quiz

Here are some pictures of musical instruments. Draw a cross on the part of each instrument that vibrates to make the sound.

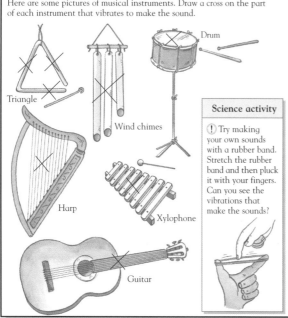

Triangle

Wind chimes

Drum

Harp

Xylophone

Guitar

Science activity

(!) Try making your own sounds with a rubber band. Stretch the rubber band and then pluck it with your fingers. Can you see the vibrations that make the sounds?

Your child will learn that sounds are made when objects vibrate. It is easy to see where sound comes from when plucked guitar strings vibrate. But the vibrations of xylophone bars are not visible, making the source of the sound harder to understand.

How are sounds changed?

Science facts

The faster an object vibrates, the higher the sound it makes. The slower an object vibrates, the lower the sound it makes. The speed at which a guitar string, drum skin or column of air in a recorder vibrates is called its pitch. Musical instruments have a high pitch or a low pitch.

Science quiz

Look at these musical instruments. Draw a line from each instrument to the way you change its pitch.

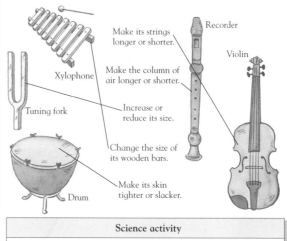

Recorder

Make its strings longer or shorter.

Xylophone

Make the column of air longer or shorter.

Tuning fork

Violin

Increase or reduce its size.

Change the size of its wooden bars.

Make its skin tighter or slacker.

Drum

Science activity

Hold a ruler on the edge of a table and twang it to make it vibrate. What sound do you get when only a little of the ruler sticks out over the table edge? What sound do you get when a lot of the ruler sticks out over the edge?

Making an object vibrate faster will increase the pitch of the sound it makes. Making it vibrate more slowly will lower the pitch. In the *Science activity*, the more of the ruler that projects over the table's edge, the lower the pitch of the twang.

What makes sound louder?

Science facts

If you hit a cymbal softly, it makes a quiet sound. If you hit it hard, it makes a loud sound. The harder you pluck a guitar string, the louder the sound it makes. The harder you blow a whistle, the louder the sound it makes. All musical instruments work in the same way.

Science quiz

Earl put some grains of rice on the skin of a tambourine. When he beat the tambourine, the rice jumped up and down as the skin vibrated.

What do you think happened to the rice grains when Earl beat the tambourine harder?

...................**They jumped higher.**...................

Science activity

You can make a simple instrument called a kazoo by folding tissue paper over the teeth of a comb. To play the kazoo, you press it to your mouth and hum through it with pursed lips. How can you make the kazoo produce a louder sound?

Your child will learn how to change the volume of a sound. Beating a tambourine harder makes the vibrations larger and so increases the volume of the sound. However, it does not change the number or speed of the vibrations, so the pitch stays the same.

How does sound travel?

Science facts

When a person sings, the vocal cords in the throat make the air vibrate. These vibrations travel through the air to your ears. You hear the vibrating air as sounds. Try feeling the vibrations in your throat when you sing. Sound can only travel as vibrations.

Science quiz

Here are two children using a string telephone. The sentences below explain how the boy can hear the girl speak, but they are jumbled up. Write the numbers 1 to 5 in the boxes to show what the correct order should be.

3 The string vibrates.

5 The vibrations are heard by the ear.

1 The girl's vocal cords vibrate.

2 The air vibrates in the girl's yogurt pot.

4 The air vibrates in the boy's yogurt pot.

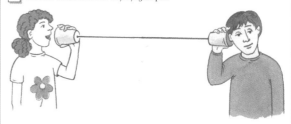

Science activity

(!) Can you make a spaghetti telephone? Use two yogurt pots and some long strands of dry spaghetti to connect them. Ask an adult to help you make a small hole in the base of each pot to insert the spaghetti. Be careful, as spaghetti breaks easily.

Sound requires a medium through which to travel to the ear. It will travel through air, string, metal, wood, glass, plastic, water, rock and any other medium that will vibrate. Even spaghetti can be used as the medium, as the *Science activity* shows.